Investment Formulas:

A Simple Introduction

Also by K.H. Erickson

Simple Introductions

Accounting and Finance Formulas
Choice Theory
Corporate Finance Formulas
eBay
Econometrics
Economics
Financial Economics
Financial Risk Management
Game Theory
Game Theory for Business
Investment Appraisal
Investment Formulas
Marketing Management Concepts and Tools
Mathematical Formulas for Economics and Business
Methods of Microeconomics
Microeconomics

Investment Formulas:

A Simple Introduction

K.H. Erickson

© 2014 K.H. Erickson

All rights reserved.

No part of this publication may be reproduced, stored in or introduced into a retrieval system, or transmitted in any form or by any means, including electronic, mechanical, photocopying, recording or otherwise, without the prior permission of the author.

Contents

Historical Return Measures	6
Investment Models	9
Portfolio Performance Evaluation	13
Firm and Stock Valuation	19
Bond Portfolio Management	22
Derivatives	27
Option Valuation	31

Historical Return Measures

Holding period returns

**Holding period return, HPR
= End value of investment / Start value of investment**

If HPR > 1 the investment generated a profit, and if HPR < 1 then the investment generated a loss.

Holding period yield, HPY = HPR − 1

The HPY value reveals an investment's percentage return.

An adjusted HPY may be used if there are interim investment contributions during the investment period:

**Adjusted HPY
= [End value of investment − ((1 − Contribution weight) x Contribution)] / [Start value of investment + (Contribution weight x Contribution)**

Contribution weight = percentage of the total investment period which the interim contribution was held.

Annual holding period returns

With HPR and HPY values the annual holding period return or annual holding period yield can be found:

Annual HPR = $HPR^{1/n}$

n = the length of the investment period in number of years.

Annual HPY = Annual HPR − 1

Mean returns

A geometric mean yield is calculated using annual HPR:

Geometric mean, GM = $[\Pi HPR]^{1/n} - 1$

n = the number of years of annual HPR data values;
Π = the product of all values being assessed;
$\Pi HPR = (HPR_1) \times (HPR_2) \times (HPR_3) \times \ldots \times (HPR_n)$.

The arithmetic mean yield is calculated with annual HPY:

Arithmetic mean, AM = $\sum HPY/n$

$\sum$ = the sum of all values being assessed;
$\sum HPY = (HPY_1) + (HPY_2) + (HPY_3) + \ldots + (HPY_n)$.

Holding period risk

Variance risk, $\sigma^2 = \sum[HPY_i - E(HPY)]^2 /n$

Standard deviation risk, $\sigma = \sqrt{\sigma^2}$
Standard deviation risk, $\sigma = \sqrt{\{\sum[HPY_i - E(HPY)]^2 /n\}}$

HPY_i = holding period yield for period i (i = 1, …, n);
$E(HPY)$ = expected HPY, i.e. the arithmetic mean HPY.

Investment Models

Abnormal returns

Abnormal returns are those returns which exceed the market return, or which exceed the expected return:

$$AR_{it} = R_{it} - R_{mt}$$

$$AR_{it} = R_{it} - E(R_{it})$$

AR_{it} = abnormal rate of return on asset i over period t;
R_{it} = return on asset i over period t;
R_{mt} = return on the market index over period t;
$E(R_{it})$ = expected return on asset i over period t.

Capital asset pricing model (CAPM)

$$E(R_i) = R_f + \beta_i[E(R_m) - R_f]$$

$E(R_i)$ = expected return on asset i;

R_f = risk-free rate of return (e.g. government bond return);
β_i = the beta of asset i, which represents the asset's sensitivity to changes in the returns of the market index. Beta value > 1 magnifies the effect of market return fluctuations, beta < 1 reduces the effect, while beta = 1 means the asset moves in exact correlation with the market. Beta is the systematic non-diversifiable risk;
$E(R_m)$ = expected return on the market index;
$[E(R_m) - R_f]$ = the market risk premium, the excess return of the market index over the risk-free rate of return.

Arbitrage pricing theory (APT)

Arbitrage pricing theory (APT) is similar to the CAPM, but instead of only one risk factor (i.e. the market index with the CAPM) affecting returns APT uses an 'n' number of risk factors:

$$E(R_i) = R_f + b_{i1} + RP_1 + b_{i2} + RP_2 + \ldots + b_{in} + RP_n$$

RP_j = the risk premium related to the jth risk factor (j = 1, ..., n);
b_{ij} = a sensitivity factor showing the relationship between the jth risk factor and asset i (j = 1, ..., n). The b_i values could be seen as performing a similar role to beta values.

Empirical factor models

The following investment return models can be calculated using an econometric regression:

$$R_{it} = \alpha_i + \beta_i R_{mt} + \varepsilon_{it}$$

α_i = the alpha/constant/intercept value in the regression;
β_i = the beta/variable/slope value in the regression;
ε_{it} = the error term, representing the difference between the return predicted by alpha and beta values and the actual return for asset i at time t.

The next model replaces returns with risk-adjusted returns, or excess returns, by subtracting the risk-free rate:

$$(R_{it} - R_{ft}) = \alpha_i + \beta_i(R_{mt} - R_{ft}) + \varepsilon_{it}$$

R_{ft} = the risk-free rate of return over period t;
$(R_{it} - R_{ft})$ = excess return of asset i over period t.

The macroeconomic model of Chen, Roll and Ross (1986) uses macroeconomic factors to explain returns:

$$R_{it} = \alpha_i + [b_{i1}R_{mt} + b_{i2}MP_t + b_{i3}I_t + b_{i4}UI_t + b_{i5}UPR_t + b_{i6}UTS_t] + \varepsilon_{it}$$

MP_t = industry monthly production growth over period t;
I_t = change in inflation (consumer price index) for period t;
UI_t = unexpected inflation, the difference between expected and actual inflation levels over period t;
UPR_t = unexpected premium returns, the change in bond credit spread (Baa bond yield – risk-free rate) for period t;
UTS_t = unexpected term structure shift (long-term risk-free rate – short-term risk-free rate) over period t.

The microeconomic model of Fama and French (1993) uses microeconomic factors to explain excess returns:

$$(R_{it} - R_{ft}) = α_i + b_{i1}(R_{mt} - R_{ft}) + b_{i2}SMB_t + b_{i3}HML_t + ε_{it}$$

SMB_t = small minus big value, the return on small capitalization stocks minus the return on large capitalization stocks over period t;
HML_t = high minus low value, the return on high book-to-market value stocks minus the return on low book-to-market value stocks over period t;

Carhart (1997) adds a momentum factor to above model:

$$(R_{it} - R_{ft}) = α_i + b_{i1}(R_{mt} - R_{ft}) + b_{i2}SMB_t + b_{i3}HML_t + b_{i4}PR1YR_t + ε_{it}$$

$PR1YR_t$ = prior 1 year return momentum trend of period t.

Portfolio Performance Evaluation

Composite portfolio performance measures

Treynor performance measure, $T = E(R_i) - E(R_f) / \beta_i$

$E(R_i)$ = expected rate of return for portfolio i (mean rate of return for portfolio i over a specified period);
$E(R_f)$ = expected risk-free rate of return for portfolio i (mean risk-free rate of return for portfolio i over a period);
$E(R_i) - E(R_f)$ = expected excess return of portfolio i over the risk-free rate of return;
β_i = the beta of portfolio i, representing the volatility of portfolio i relative to market volatility. Beta represents systematic non-diversifiable risk only and ignores non-systematic diversifiable risk.

Sharpe performance measure, $S = E(R_i) - E(R_f) / \sigma_i$

σ_i = the standard deviation (SD) of portfolio i. SD is a measure of total risk, including both systematic non-diversifiable risk, and non-systematic diversifiable risk.

Jensen performance measure
$= (R_{it} - R_{ft}) = α_i + β_i[R_{mt} - R_{ft}] + ε_{it}$

R_{it} = the rate return of portfolio i over the specific time period t;
R_{ft} = the risk-free rate of return over time t;
$(R_{it} - R_{ft})$ = the excess rate of return of portfolio i over the risk-free rate of return over time period t;
R_{mt} = the return of the market index portfolio, m, for time period t;
$(R_{mt} - R_{ft})$ = the excess rate of return of the market portfolio over the risk-free rate of return at time t;
$α_i$ = an investment manager's ability to make above-average risk-adjusted returns using stock selection or market timing techniques with portfolio i. The value of $α_i$, also known as alpha, can be found using a regression where $(R_{it} - R_{ft})$ is the dependent or y variable and $(R_{mt} - R_{ft})$ is the independent or x variable. A positive and statistically significant $α_i$ value signals superior performance from an investment manager, while a negative and statistically significant $α_i$ value signals inferior performance. A zero or statistically insignificant value suggests the manager's portfolio performance was neither superior nor inferior to what would be expected;
$ε_{it}$ = the error in the calculated relationship between $(R_{it} - R_{ft})$ and $(R_{mt} - R_{ft})$ for portfolio i over time period t.

Information ratio performance measure, IR_i
$= E(R_i) - E(R_b) / \sigma_{ER} = E(ER_i) / \sigma_{ER}$

IR_i = the information ratio for portfolio i;
$E(R_i)$ = expected rate of return for portfolio i (mean rate of return for portfolio i over a specified period);
$E(R_b)$ = expected rate of return for benchmark portfolio b (mean rate of return for benchmark portfolio over period);
$E(ER_i) = E(R_i) - E(R_b)$ = the excess rate of return of portfolio i over the rate of return of benchmark portfolio b;
σ_{ER} = the standard deviation of the excess return over the specified period, known as the portfolio's tracking error.

The Jensen and information ratio performances measures can be combined to give a simplified IR measure:

Information ratio performance measure, $IR_i = \alpha_i / \sigma_\varepsilon$

α_i = the Jensen portfolio performance measure alpha value;
σ_ε = standard deviation of the regression's error term, ε.

This simplified IR performance measure can be turned into an annualized IR measure with the following formula:

Annualized IR $= (T)\alpha_i / (\sqrt{T})\sigma_\varepsilon = (\sqrt{T})IR_i$

T = number of times per year returns were measured.

Components of portfolio performance

The overall performance of a portfolio manager in earning an excess return over the risk-free rate can be divided into separate security selection and risk-taking components:

Overall performance = Excess return = Selectivity + Portfolio risk

$$(R_i - R_f) = [R_i - R_p(\beta_i)] + [R_p(\beta_i) - R_f]$$

$(R_i - R_f)$ = excess return rate of portfolio i over the risk-free rate of return;

$R_p(\beta_i)$ = the return on a passive buy and hold investment strategy portfolio combining a risk-free asset and the market index, R_p, which is associated with a systematic risk level of β_p which equals the risk of portfolio i, β_i;

$[R_i - R_p(\beta_i)]$ = the excess return of portfolio i over the return of the passive buy and hold portfolio p combining a risk-free asset and the market index, which has the same level of systematic risk. This represents the excess return a portfolio manager achieves without increasing the level of risk, and highlights the manager's security selectivity skill;

$[R_p(\beta_i) - R_f]$ = the excess return of the passive buy and hold portfolio p over the risk-free rate. As the passive buy and hold portfolio p has the same risk as portfolio i this reveals what the excess return of portfolio i over the risk-free rate is expected to be, and the return which taking on additional portfolio risk would be expected to generate if the investment manager had zero security selectivity skill.

Selectivity minus diversification equals net selectivity:

Net selectivity = Selectivity − Diversification

Net selectivity = $[R_i - R_p(\beta_i)] - [R_p(\sigma(R_i)) - R_p(\beta_i)]$

$R_p(\sigma(R_i))$ = the return on a passive buy and hold investment strategy portfolio combining a risk-free asset and the market index, R_p, with a return dispersion of $\sigma(R_p)$ which equals the return dispersion of portfolio i, $\sigma(R_i)$;

$[R_p(\sigma(R_i)) - R_p(\beta_i)]$ = the diversification measure, which represents the level of added return required to justify any sacrifice of diversification in the portfolio. In a fully diversified portfolio $\sigma = \beta$, and the diversification measure will equal zero to ensure net selectivity = selectivity.

Performance attribution

Total value added = Allocation effect + Selection effect

Allocation effect = $\sum_i [(w_{ai} - w_{bi}) \times (R_{bi} - R_b)]$

Selection effect = $\sum_i [(w_{ai}) \times (R_{ai} - R_{bi})]$

$\sum_i$ = summation for all values of i;
w_{ai} = weight of market segment i in the investment manager's actual portfolio;
w_{bi} = weight of market segment i in the benchmark portfolio;
R_{ai} = return of market segment i in the investment manager's actual portfolio;
R_{bi} = return of market segment i in the benchmark portfolio;
R_b = total return of the benchmark portfolio.

Firm and Stock Valuation

Growth models

The value of a firm can be measured using a growth model. If a firm has no growth its value (V_{NG}) is:

$V_{NG} = E / k$

E = constant net earnings stream after depreciation;
k = required rate of return.

The no growth model of firm valuation assumes all earnings are paid out in dividends, with a retention rate of zero:

$V_{NG} = (1 - ret)E / k$

ret = retention rate of earnings.

It's assumed that the rate of return, r = k, the required rate of return, and investors receive k from their investment:

$k = E / V_{NG}$

Long-run growth models differ from no-growth models as they assume that some of a firm's earnings are reinvested, instead of all being paid out in dividends, with a retention rate above zero. A growth firm's valuation (V_G) is:

$$V_G = [(1 - ret)E / k] + (ret)Em / k$$

E = the level of constant net earnings after depreciation expected from current investments, without additional net investments;
m = is the relative rate of return on reinvestments and in the reinvestment model r = mk. If m = 1 then r = k (rate of return = required rate of return), but if m > 1 then r > k and the associated project investments are true growth investments which generate excess returns. And if m < 1 then r < k and the investments generate returns below the cost of capital and are therefore not economically viable.

Value added

Value added measures evaluate investment performance:

Economic value added, EVA = NOPAT − D

NOPAT = net operating profit after tax;

D, dollar cost of capital = WACC x C;
C = capital assets invested;
WACC = weighted average cost of capital.

WACC = (Cost of equity x Weight of equity) + (Cost of debt after tax x Weight of debt)

WACC = $\{k_E \times [V_E / (V_E + V_D)]\} + \{k_D \times (1 - T_C) \times [V_D / (V_E + V_D)]\}$

k_E = market cost of equity;
k_D = cost of debt;
V_E = book value of equity;
V_D = book value of debt;
T_C = corporate tax rate;
$(1 - T_C)$ = after tax.

Market value added, MVA = Market value of firm − C − Market value of debt − Market value of equity

Share valuation

Fund net asset value, NAV = (Total market value of fund portfolio − Fund expenses) / Total outstanding fund shares

Bond Portfolio Management

Bond returns

$HPR_{it} = (P_{it+1} + i_{it}) / P_{it}$

HPR_{it} = holding period return on bond i over period t;
P_{it+1} = market price of bond i at the end of period t;
P_{it} = market price of bond i at the start of period t;
i_{it} = interest made on bond i over period t.

The interest income on some bonds is tax-exempt. To compare the yields offered by such bonds with regular taxable bonds a fully taxable equivalent yield is used:

Fully taxable equivalent yield, $FTEY = i_{TE} / (1 - MT)$

i_{TE} = yield promised on the tax-exempt bond;
MT = investor's marginal tax rate.

The interest rate plays a major role in a bond's returns, and it is calculated as follows:

Interest rate, $i = R_f + I + RP$

R_f = real risk-free rate of interest;
I = expected inflation rate;
RP = risk premium.

Bond price-yield relationship

Macaulay duration measures the timing of cash flows from a bond, assuming annual compounding:

Macaulay Duration, $D = \sum[C_t(t) / (1+i)^t] / \sum[C_t / (1+i)^t]$

C_t = principal or coupon cash flow at time period t;
t = the time period (i.e. the year number) when the principal or coupon cash flow payment occurs;
i = the bond's yield to maturity.

Macaulay duration can also be found more directly:

$$D = [(1 + i/n) / (i/n)] - \{(1 + i/n + [(n \times T)(C/P - i/n)]) / (C/P[(1 + i/n)^{n \times T} - 1] + i/n)\}$$

n = number of payments per year;
T = number of years to maturity;
C = periodic coupon payment;
P = principal or face value paid at maturity.

Macaulay duration can be adjusted to give a modified duration measure, which approximates the interest rate sensitivity of a bond without options:

Modified duration, $D_M = D / (1 + i/n)$

Modified duration can then be used to estimate changes in price following yield changes:

D_M estimated price change, $\Delta P = -D_M \times \%\Delta i \times$ Bond price

ΔP = change in price;
$\%\Delta i$ = basis point percentage change in yield. e.g. if the yield changes from 3% to 4% the $\%\Delta i = 1\% = 0.01$;
Bond price = sum of the present value of cash flows, i.e. $\sum [C_t / (1 + i)^t]$.

Modified duration is only accurate for very small changes in yield as it assumes a linear relationship between yield and price, when the actual price-yield curve is convex. A convexity measure corrects for the inaccuracy of modified duration:

Convexity = (d^2P / di^2) / Bond price

$d^2P / di^2 = 1 / (1 + i)^2 \; [\sum (t^2 + t) \, C_t / (1 + i)^t]$

The convexity value can be used to give the convexity estimated price change:

Convexity estimated price change = 0.5 x Convexity x (%Δi)² x Bond price

The convexity estimated price change is then added to the modified duration estimated price change for the total estimated price change following a yield change.

Total estimated price change after a yield change = Modified duration estimated price change + Convexity estimated price change

Bonds with call or put options

Earlier duration and convexity measures are for option-free bonds only, and if bonds have embedded options the analysis changes. A bond with a call option gives the owner the right, but not the obligation, to buy the bond at a specific time at a specific price. A bond with a put option gives the owner the right, but not the obligation, to sell the bond at a specific time at a specific price. The following equations note the impact of these options:

Callable bond price = Non-callable bond price − Call option price

Putable bond value = Non-putable bond value − Put option value

Option-adjusted duration = Duration of non-callable bond − duration of call option

There are also new duration and convexity measures which account for bonds with embedded options, called effective duration and effective convexity respectively:

Effective Duration (D_E) = (P^- − P^+) / (2 × P × S)

Effective Convexity (C_E) = (P^- + P^+ − 2P) / (P × S^2)

P^- = estimated bond price after downward interest rate shift;
P^+ = estimated bond price after upward interest rate shift;
P = current price of bond before any interest rate shifts;
S = shift in term structure of interest rates in basis percentage points.

Derivatives

Put-call spot parity

The relationship between the current value of a stock, put option, call option, and risk-free Treasury bill is summarized by the put-call spot parity. The parity holds for European style options which can only be exercised at maturity:

$$S_0 + P_{0,T} - C_{0,T} = X / (1 + R_f)^T$$

S_0 = current stock value (i.e. value at time zero);
$P_{0,T}$ = current value of put option which expires at time T;
$C_{0,T}$ = current value of call option which expires at time T;
T = expiration or maturity time;
X = principal or face value of a risk-free zero coupon bond (e.g. T-bill) which matures at time T = exercise price.

The above equation can be rewritten in financial terms:

(Long stock) + (Long put) + (Short call) = (Long T-bill)

Long = buy the asset, as a price rise is expected;

Short = sell the asset, as a price fall is expected, with the intention of buying the asset back at a future lower price.

The inverse of the previous two equations also holds:

$-S_0 - P_{0,T} + C_{0,T} = - X / (1 + R_f)^T$

(Short stock) + (Short put) + (Long call) = (Short T-bill)

Creating synthetic securities using the put-call spot parity

The put-call spot parity can be rearranged to show how a synthetic stock, risk-free asset, put option, or call option can be created using the other three. A synthetic stock or risk-free T-bill asset is created with the following method:

$S_0 = [X / (1 + R_f)^T] - P_{0,T} + C_{0,T}$

(Long stock) = (Long T-bill) + (Short put) + (Long call)

$[X / (1 + R_f)^T] = S_0 + P_{0,T} - C_{0,T}$

(Long T-bill) = (Long stock) + (Long put) + (Short call)

And a synthetic call or put option can be created as shown by the following equations:

$$C_{0,T} = S_0 + P_{0,T} - [X / (1 + R_f)^T]$$

(Long call) = (Long stock) + (Long put) + (Short T-bill)

$$P_{0,T} = [X / (1 + R_f)^T] - S_0 + C_{0,T}$$

(Long put) = (Long T-bill) + (Short stock) + (Long call)

Put-call spot parity with dividends

If stocks have dividends then the put-call spot parity changes. An additional variable which accounts for the discounted value of dividends is added to the model:

$$S_0 - [D_T / (1 + R_f)^T] + P_{0,T} - C_{0,T} = X / (1 + R_f)^T$$

(Long stock) + (Short present value of dividends) + (Long put) + (Short call) = (Long T-bill)

D_T = the dividend paid just before the asset's expiration date, T.

Put-call forward parity

While the put-call spot parity examines current (spot) relationships between assets, an alternative put-call forward parity is required to show the relationship between assets at a future time. The put-call forward parity replaces the current stock, S_0, with a forward contract discounted to give its present value, $[F_{0,T} / (1 + R_f)^T]$:

$$[F_{0,T} / (1 + R_f)^T] + P_{0,T} - C_{0,T} + = X / (1 + R_f)^T$$

(Long forward contract) + (Long put) + (Short call) = (Long T-bill)

$F_{0,T}$ = current value of a forward contract which expires at time T. A forward contract is an agreement between two parties to buy or sell an asset at a specific price at a specific future time.

The relationship between spot (S_0) and forward rates (F_0):

$$S_0 = F_{0,T} / (1 + R_f)^T$$

With dividends the spot to forward relationship becomes:

$$S_0 - [D_T / (1 + R_f)^T] = F_{0,T} / (1 + R_f)^T$$

Option Valuation

Black-Scholes formula for call option valuation

The Black-Scholes model assumes that stock prices follow a geometric Brownian motion, which is a continuous but random process with drift and volatility:

Stock return = $\mu[\Delta T] + \sigma\varepsilon[\Delta T]^{1/2}$

T = expiration date;
Δ = change;
μ = mean return, the percentage drift;
σ = standard deviation, the percentage volatility;
ε = random error term;
$\mu[\Delta T]$ = expected aspect of stock return;
$\sigma\varepsilon[\Delta T]^{1/2}$ = unexpected 'noise' aspect of stock return.

The Black-Scholes model values a European style (only exercised at maturity) call option on a stock without dividends, assuming a constant continuously compounded risk-free rate and stock variance:

$C_0 = SN(d_1) - X(e^{-(Rf)T})N(d_2)$

$d_1 = [(Ln(S/X) + (R_f + 0.5\sigma^2)[T])] / (\sigma[T]^{1/2})$

$d_2 = d_1 - \sigma[T]^{1/2}$

C_0 = value of a call option at the current time (time zero);
S = stock price;
N(d) = cumulative probability of seeing a value drawn from a standard normal distribution (i.e. mean = 0, σ = 1);
X = face value paid at maturity = exercise price;
e = exponential function, inverse of the natural logarithm;
R_f = risk-free rate.
Ln = natural logarithm, inverse of exponential function;
σ^2 = variance.

$N(d) \approx 0.5e^{-(d \times d)/2 - 281/(83 - 351/d)}$ if $d < 0$
$N(d) \approx 1 - 0.5e^{-(d \times d)/2 - 281/(83 + 351/d)}$ if $d \geq 0$

Black-Scholes put option valuation

The value of a European put option was given earlier as:

$P_{0,T} = [X / (1 + R_f)^T] - S_0 + C_{0,T}$

If the discounting process for the risk-free T-bill asset is turned into a continuous function, as the Black-Scholes model uses with its assumption of a geometric Brownian motion, the value of a European style put option becomes:

$$P_0 = X(e^{-(Rf)T}) - S + C_0$$

P_0 = value of a put option at the current time (time zero).

Combining this with the Black-Scholes formula for a call option C_0 gives the following value for a put option:

$$P_0 = X(e^{-(Rf)T}) - S + [SN(d_1) - X(e^{-(Rf)T})N(d_2)]$$

And this can be manipulated to create the following Black-Scholes put valuation model:

$$P_0 = X(e^{-(Rf)T})N(-d_2) - SN(-d_1)$$

Black-Scholes formula with dividends

Call option dividends changes the Black-Scholes formula:

$$C_0 = (e^{-(D)T})SN(d_1) - X(e^{-(Rf)T})N(d_2)$$

$$d_1 = [(Ln((e^{-(D)T})S/X) + (R_f + 0.5\sigma^2)[T])] / (\sigma[T]^{1/2})$$
$$d_2 = d_1 - \sigma[T]^{1/2}$$

www.ingramcontent.com/pod-product-compliance
Lightning Source LLC
Chambersburg PA
CBHW070729180526
45167CB00004B/1684